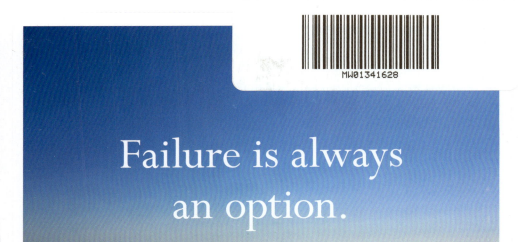

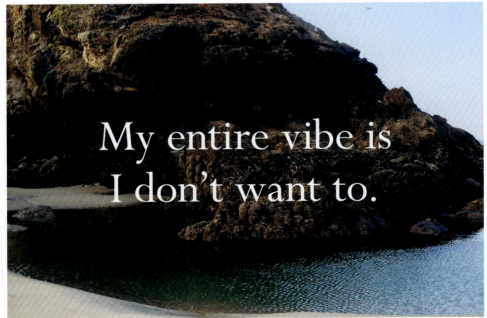

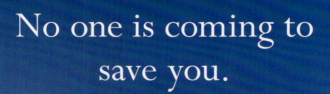

No one is coming to save you.

You are the adult.

I am so sorry.

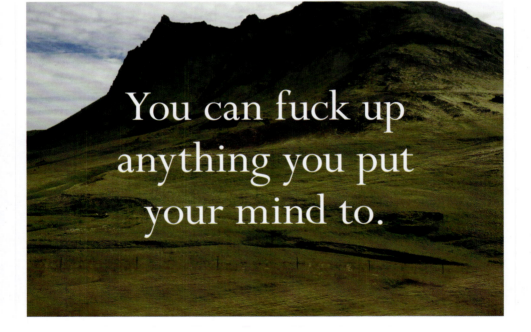

You can fuck up anything you put your mind to.

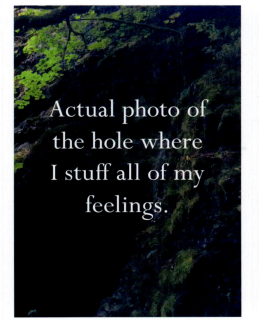
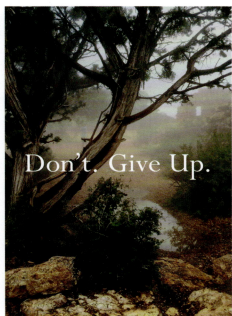

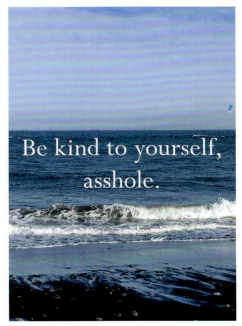

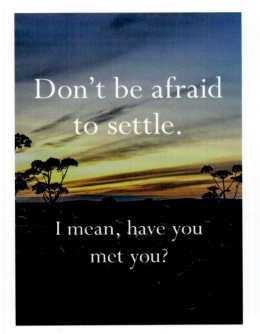
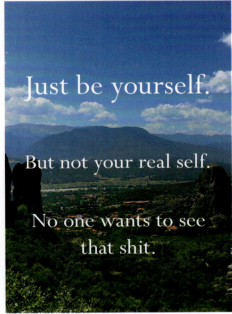
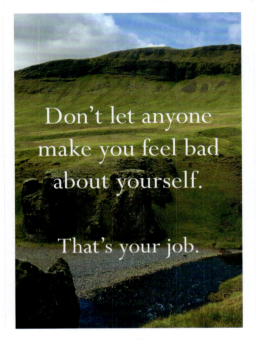
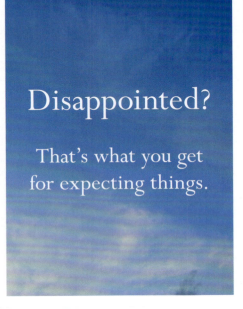

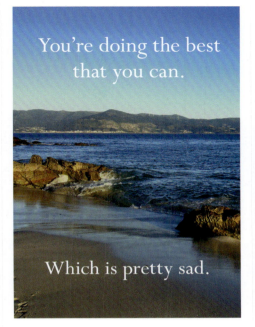
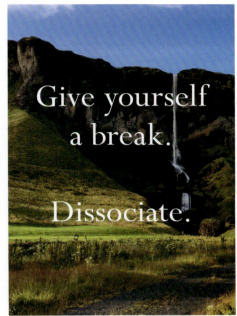

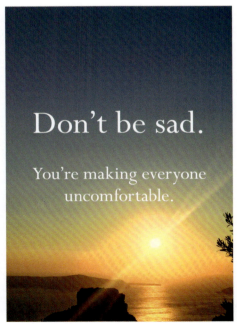

You matter.

Just not that much.

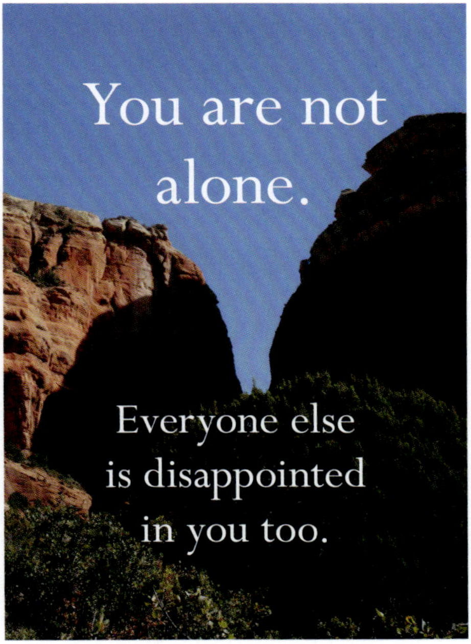

You are not alone.

Everyone else is disappointed in you too.

I will not lose control of my emotions.

I lost that shit a long time ago.

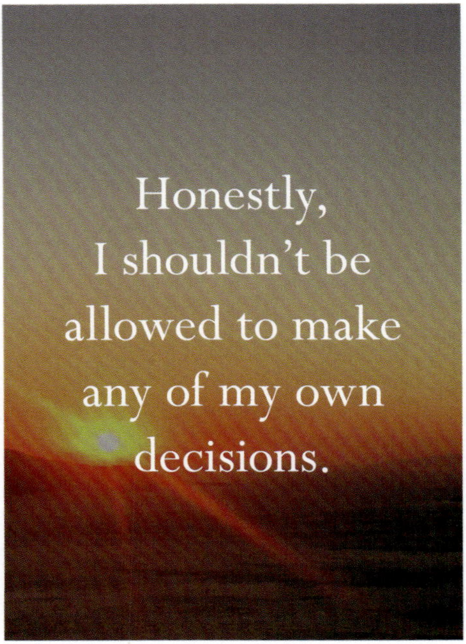

Honestly, I shouldn't be allowed to make any of my own decisions.

It's never too
late to change.

So just wait until you
absolutely have to.

Each new day is a
gift you can't return
for something that
you really want.

No one is coming to
save you.

You are the adult.

I am so sorry.

It's not imposter
syndrome.

You really do
suck at
everything.

Have a panic attack. You've earned it.	Things didn't work out for a reason. The reason is you.
I am exactly where I want to be. At home, avoiding people.	I am only saying yes to things that spark joy. If only I ever felt any joy.

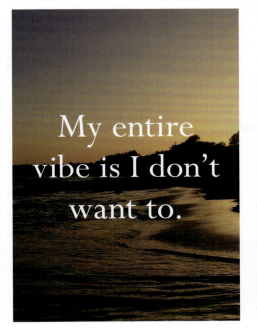

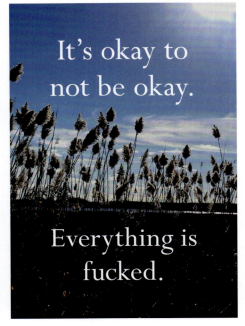

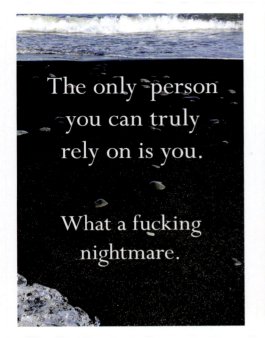

The only person you can truly rely on is you.

What a fucking nightmare.

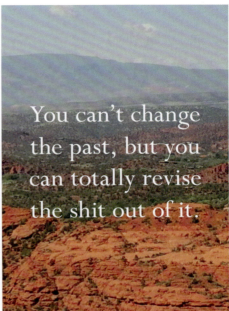

You can't change the past, but you can totally revise the shit out of it.

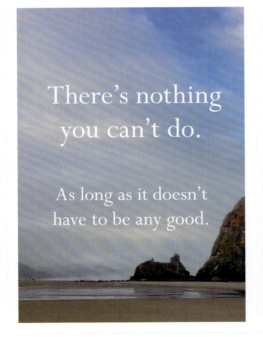

There's nothing you can't do.

As long as it doesn't have to be any good.

Let go of the past.

You're holding yourself back from making new regrets.

It's okay to have feelings.

But do you need to have so many?

Every now and then, scream at the top of your lungs. It helps.

Fuck it, take a nap.

Ask the universe for guidance.

Then do the stupid shit you were going to do anyway.

Self-Sabotage

Why wait for things to fail when you can make it happen?

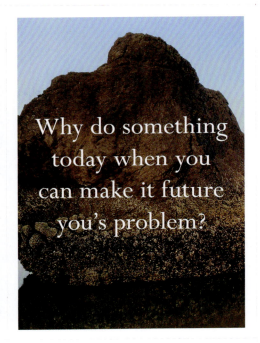

Why do something today when you can make it future you's problem?

Unfollow your dreams!

Today I am putting myself first.

If that's okay with you.

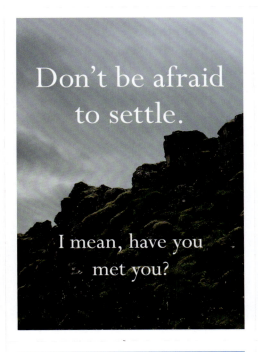

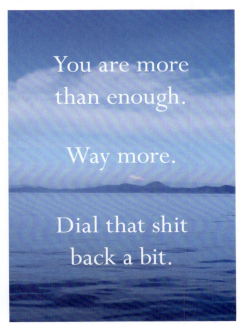

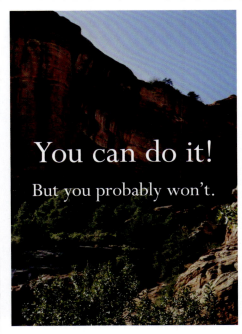

Failure is always an option.

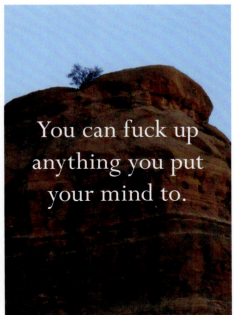

You can fuck up anything you put your mind to.

Accept yourself for the hot mess that you are.

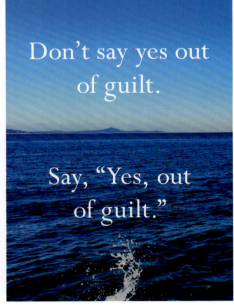

Don't say yes out of guilt.

Say, "Yes, out of guilt."

Let go of the past.

You're holding yourself back from making new regrets.

You are more than enough.

Way more.

Dial that shit back a little bit.

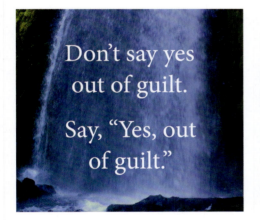

Don't say yes out of guilt.

Say, "Yes, out of guilt."

Disappointed?

That's what you get for expecting things.

Be proud of how far you've come.

Especially by only doing the bare minimum.

Stop overthinking.

You are the only one who cares.

Each new day is a gift you can't return for something you really want.

It gets easier.

Eventually you just stop giving a fuck.

Give yourself a break.

Disassociate.

Self-Sabotage

Why wait for things to fail when you can make it happen?

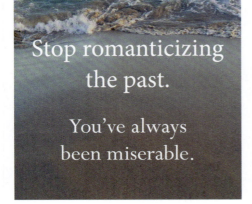

Stop romanticizing the past.

You've always been miserable.

You are not alone.

Everyone else is disappointed in you too.

My entire vibe is I don't want to.	Why do something today when you can make it future you's problem?
You can't change the past, but you can totally revise the shit out of it.	It's okay to have feelings. But do you need to have so many?
Accept yourself for the hot mess that you are.	Honestly, I shouldn't be allowed to make any of my own decisions.

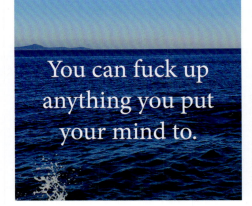

Today I am putting myself first. If that's okay with you.	Just be yourself. But not your real self. No one wants to see that shit.
It's not imposter syndrome. You really do suck at everything.	Mistakes are how we learn. I keep getting better at them.
You're doing the best you can. Which is pretty sad.	Failure is always an option.

You matter. Just not that much.	**Be kind to yourself, asshole.**
You attract the energy that you give off. Apparently I only give off weird vibes.	**It's okay to not be okay.** **Everything is fucked.**
I will not lose control of my emotions. I lost that shit a long time ago.	**Have a panic attack. You've earned it.**

Don't be sad.
You're making everyone uncomfortable.

Failure is always an option.

The only person you can truly rely on is you.
What a fucking nightmare.

You can do it!
But you probably won't.

Fuck it, take a nap.

Not every day is precious.
Waste today. You deserve it.

Things didn't work out for a reason. The reason is you.

Unfollow your dreams!

My entire vibe is I don't want to.

It's not imposter syndrome.
You really do suck at everything.

Accept yourself for the hot mess that you are.

Honestly, I shouldn't be allowed to make any of my own decisions.

Stop overthinking. You are the only one who cares.	**Don't. Give Up.**
You matter. Just not that much.	**It's okay to not be okay.** Everything's fucked.
Stop romanticizing the past. You've always been miserable.	Today I am putting myself first. If that's okay with you.
You can fuck up anything you put your mind to.	Be kind to yourself, asshole.
You're doing the best you can. Which is pretty sad.	Give yourself a break. Disassociate.
Have a panic attack. You've earned it.	It gets easier. Eventually you stop giving a fuck.